# Young
# Shakespeare

# Young Shakespeare

## Tony Bonning

### Illustrated by Gillian Alexander

WAVERLEY
BOOKS

# ACKNOWLEDGEMENTS

Special thanks to The Shakespeare Trust and to guide, John Colton, whose knowledge of Shakespeare and his time is encyclopaedic.

**TONY BONNING**

Published 2009 by Waverley Books,
David Dale House, New Lanark, ML11 9DJ, Scotland

Text © Tony Bonning 2009

Illustrations by Gillian Alexander

Young Classics is a trademark of Waverley Books

ISBN 978 1 902407 42 5

Printed and bound in Poland

# DEDICATION

Dedicated to Ross and Andrew Coleman Davis:
real heroes.

# CONTENTS

# YOUNG SHAKESPEARE

## The Elizabethan world

Often when we look at history and historical people we measure their lives according to our own. We wonder how they managed without electricity and running water, cars and televisions, hospitals and doctors. We might even feel sorry for them that they did not have these things. The fact is that they had no idea of these things so could not miss them! Without them, they saw the world in a totally different way from us. In fact, the way people saw the world in William Shakespeare's time was so different from ours that they might as well have been from another planet as from another time.

The 16th century is one of the most important crossroads in history. The Middle Ages or medieval times were at an end, America and the New World had been discovered and the companions of Ferdinand Magellan had proved that the world was round (Magellan had been killed during their incredible sea journey).

England under Elizabeth I was obtaining great wealth from the discovery of the Americas, mainly by the piracy of Spanish vessels. Its great heroes were Sir Francis Drake, who famously trashed the Spanish Armada, and Sir Walter Raleigh, who introduced potatoes and tobacco to this country – something to help the people live longer and something to kill them off!

Also, the Reformation was in full swing, with people protesting against the power of the Roman Catholic Church. The reformers said that the Roman Catholic Church had kept the people of Europe steeped in ignorance and superstition. In many cases they just replaced it with more ignorance and superstition.

However, the Reformation opened the way for the Age of Reason and the development of science. Under Elizabeth I, England was a Protestant country in name, though there were many, like Shakespeare's family, who still had sympathy for the old Roman Catholic faith.

Elizabethans believed that the universe was structured in the *Scala Naturae* or 'Great Chain of Being' where God was the highest being and below him the angels then humans, beasts, fish, plants and rocks.

Even the monarch was there by the will of God: by what was called 'Divine Right'. Everything was in its place and there was no equality. The phrase 'animal, vegetable and mineral' reveals a leftover from this belief that is still alive today, although originally it was 'holy, animal, vegetable and mineral'.

The population of England at the time is thought to have been just over three million, with the majority of people living out in the country. The Queen lived in London with her court; the aristocracy lived in castles and large stone-built country houses; the lesser aristocracy lived in manor houses made partly of brick and timber. Next were merchants who usually lived in towns, many of which were no bigger than some present-day villages. Their houses were generally built from timber, brick and clay, as were the houses of the wealthier farmers or yeomen.

Poor tenant farmers and peasants, who earned as little as 2p a day (now worth £1.50), lived in shacks built from clay and wattle. First stakes were placed in the ground, then willow wands (slender, supple sticks of willow) were weaved between them. The willow 'walls' were then coated with a mixture of clay, lime and dung. Roof beams were put in place, covered by branches, then turf, then a top layer of straw or thatch.

The homes of the really poor might have been made simply with turf.

## Life in Shakespeare's Stratford

In Shakespeare's time, Stratford was a small town of around 1,500 to 2,000 people. As is the case today, houses were rented or owned. Instead of council tax, you paid money to the major landowner who for the town of Stratford was the Bishop of Worcester. A large cottage like Shakespeare's cost 13p a year and a small cottage, like the one attached to William's house, cost 12p a year – about £9.00 in today's money.

As the houses were built from timber, brick, clay and wattle, and roofed or thatched with straw, fires were not uncommon. Most thatch fires were caused by cracks in the chimney while others were caused by sparks, especially during a hot summer, as even then people kept fires going to cook on.

There were bad house fires in Stratford in 1594 and 1595 after long hot summers. One was caused by a good deed: a woman carried a firebrand into a neighbour's house so that she could light her bread oven and accidentally set the house on fire!

Evidence suggests that at that time the roof of Shakespeare's house was tiled, which made its chances of being burned down a little less likely – perhaps one of the

reasons it still stands to this day!

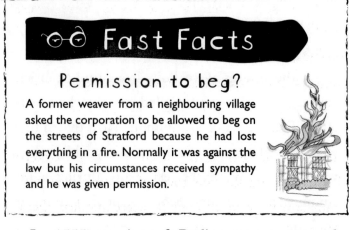

## ⊙ə Fast Facts

### Permission to beg?

A former weaver from a neighbouring village asked the corporation to be allowed to beg on the streets of Stratford because he had lost everything in a fire. Normally it was against the law but his circumstances received sympathy and he was given permission.

In 1555 an Act of Parliament was passed ordering all parishes to maintain their roads, though it would be another three hundred years before they got round to it. Country roads were just rough muddy tracks. Why bother looking after these roads when the farthest anyone would travel would only be a half-day away? The other half of the day was to get back!

Travellers, such as returning pilgrims, peddlers, soldiers back from the wars and actors, were treated with suspicion. Their only value was either the goods they sold or the tales they told. For most people, all their needs and wants were supplied locally – they grew their own food, made their own clothes and provided their own entertainment.

Town streets were a little better; some were cobbled, but in the main it was just hard-packed earth and rubble which, in the rain, turned into a mire of mud. Stratford has many wide streets; this was because in 1196 the Bishop of Worcester obtained permission from Richard I (the famous 'Richard the Lionheart') to hold street markets; because of this the new town of Stratford was built with streets wide enough to accommodate them. The main market in Shakespeare's time was at the junction of High Street and Bridge Street.

Because most people kept animals it was normal

to see ducks, geese, chickens, sheep, cows and horses in the street adding their share of the mess. It was known for people to erect pens in the street to contain them; though one man is known to have been fined for letting his ducks and pigs run loose in the street. Dogs were not allowed to run about loose and had to wear muzzles if they were out and about.

As if the mess from all these animals was not bad enough, butchers were sometimes guilty of throwing the entrails and heads of slaughtered animals out into the street!

Because of rumours of the plague, new byelaws were brought in to outlaw this practice. John Shakespeare, William's father, was himself fined for keeping a midden (muck heap) outside his door rather than removing it to the town midden at the top of Henley Street, not far from his house.

At first glance, Stratford must have seemed a peaceable enough place during Shakespeare's time. However, there was a byelaw preventing young unmarried men from carrying weapons into town, especially daggers, because of the many street brawls. These regular fights were the reason for the old custom of men walking on the outside of the pavement or sidewalk when escorting a lady: it was for protection.

Shakespeare uses street brawls in his plays, most famously in *Romeo and Juliet.*

The Elizabethan population was kept low by a high death rate through bad hygiene, poverty and regular outbreaks of the plague and other infectious diseases. The worst of these was the bubonic plague but people also suffered illnesses like smallpox and flu, which were often fatal.

Stratford suffered from the plague in the year William Shakespeare was born and about a fifth of the population died from it, including four children two doors away from Shakespeare's home.

---

## From the *Plague Pamphlets* of Thomas Dekkar

For he that durst in the dead hour of gloomy midnight have been so valiant to have walked through the still and melancholy streets – what think you then should have been his music? Surely the loud groans of raving sick men, the struggling pangs of souls departing; in every house striking up an alarum – servants crying out for masters, wives for husbands, parents for children, children for their mothers. Here, he should have met some frantically running to knock up sextons; there, others, fearfully sweating with coffins, stealing forth dead bodies lest the fatal handwriting of Death should seal up their doors. And to make this dismal concert more full, round about him bells heavily tolling in one place or ringing out in another. The dreadfulness of such an hour is unutterable.

---

On that cheery note let us now turn our attention to Young Will!

## Birth

What do we know about him? Very little, actually. If everyone knew you were going to be famous a record would be kept of your birth and childhood, as is often the case of kings and queens of old. But William didn't exactly pop out and say 'I'm going to be famous.' Or maybe he did, but to everyone else it just sounded like 'Waaaah!'

While we only have a very little information, with the right kind of detective work we can begin to build up some kind of picture. In fact, even the lack of information tells us something – we don't know exactly when he was born so that tells us that births were not recorded as they are nowadays.

We do know that he was baptised at Holy Trinity Church in 1564, for a register was kept that says:

### April 26: Gulielmus filius Johannes Shakspeare
### (William, son of John Shakespeare)

And we can be fairly certain he was born anything up to three days before that. It is suggested that he was born on 23 April – St George's Day – the same day on which he died 52 years later. This is probably too neat, though not impossible. He was the third child born to Mary Shakespeare but the first to survive childhood.

Death in childhood was all too common in Elizabethan times. Standards of cleanliness and hygiene were extremely bad and you were more likely to die from medical treatment than to survive it. Look around you in your class at school: if this was the 16th century, at least a third of your class would not be there. You would, of  course, be one of the lucky ones – you hope!

There were also threats to life from infectious diseases. Bubonic plague killed more than a fifth of the townsfolk of Stratford three months after young Shakespeare was born. If this seems far-fetched, take a look below at the lifespans of Young Will and his brothers and sisters.

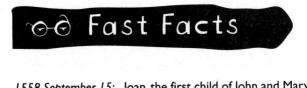

## Fast Facts

*1558 September 15:* Joan, the first child of John and Mary was baptised (she died aged two months)

*1562 December 2:* Margaret baptised (she died one year later)

*1564 April 26:* William baptised (died 1616 aged 52)

*1566 October 13:* Gilbert baptised (died 1612 aged 46)

*1569:* A daughter, also called Joan, was born (died 1646 aged 77)

*1571 September 28:* Anne baptised (died 1579 aged 7)

*1574 March 11:* Richard baptised (died 1613 aged 39)

*1580 May 3:* Edmund baptised (died 1607 aged 27)

If we can't know exactly about William Shakespeare the boy, perhaps we can begin to understand something of him through the world he was born into.

William was born in the small Warwickshire town of Stratford on the River Avon in the Forest of Arden. The name Stratford comes from the Roman name for a road or highway, 'straet' or street, and the Old English word, 'ford', meaning a river crossing. The name Avon is the Celtic word for river and Arden is from the Anglo-Saxon for a dwelling-place.

The main landowning family of the area also adopted the name Arden. William's mother, Mary Arden, was from this family. His father, John, was a glover and whittawer to trade – he made gloves and a 'whittawer' means he worked in white leather.

We know that John was a successful businessman, for in 1568 he became town bailiff or mayor. John and Mary owned a house in Henley Street that was probably bought in two stages in 1556 and 1575. It is likely, though not certain, that William was born in this house, now called 'the Birthplace'.

## Baby Will

At first the infant,
Mewling and puking in the nurse's arms.

Jacques in *As You Like It* Act 2, Scene 7

Like the baby Jesus, young Will would have been wrapped in swaddling clothes, by which we mean he was wrapped tightly with strips of linen from his neck to his feet. This would have been done for most of the first year of his life. The reason was to ensure that legs and arms grew straight. Rickets caused by a lack of vitamin D was a common ailment.

Strangely enough, the rich tended to eat badly by refusing to eat vegetables that grew beneath the soil, such as carrots. That must have pleased the children of the times! The wealthy tended to eat meat, onions, leeks and garlic.

Fruit was seldom eaten raw but rather as preserves or in pies (along with the four and twenty blackbirds for effect – true at banquets!).

On the other hand the poor generally had a good diet mainly of vegetables; sadly for many

the poverty and squalor in which they lived undid the good work of their healthy food. Everyone, and this included children, drank ale or beer as it was considered healthier than water (hic!).

The Shakespeares, coming from a middle-class family with a background in farming, would probably have enjoyed both vegetables and meat: vegetables most of the time and meat for feasts and special occasions.

For baby Will it would have been mother's milk or, as they were not poor, a wet-nurse who took over the breastfeeding. Swaddled as he was he wouldn't be able to protest too much except,

OOPS – THAT'S MY MUM *OVER THERE!* burp!

as it says on page 22, by 'mewling and puking'.

'Polonian Sawsedge' was a regular dish, because in an age before refrigerators it kept for a long time without going off. Here's the recipe:

---

### Polonian Sawsedge

Take the fillers (internal organs) of a hog; chop them very small with a handful of red sage: season it hot with ginger and pepper, and then put it in a great sheep's gut; then let it lie three nights in brine; then boil it and hang it up in a chimney where fire is usually kept; and these sawsedges will last a whole yeere. They are good for sallades or to garnish boiled meats, or to make one rellish a cup of wine.

---

Yum, yum!

## Early childhood

Strange as it may seem to us now, up until the age of five, young William would have worn a skirt the same as his younger sisters. To show the difference he would have worn a man's hat and doublet or jacket.

THOUGHT THEY SAID I WAS A BOY, NOT A GIRL.

He would have also worn diapers or nappies until then. At the age of five he would have been potty trained and undergone what was called 'breeching'. In other words, he would now wear breeches or knee-length trousers. This was a very special occasion for growing boys and was still the case in many homes right through until the 1920s.

Although it was often ignored, there was a law against people dressing in the styles and clothes not of their class, for clothes were meant to show rank and privilege.

For the aristocracy there was silk and gold jewellery; for the middle class, fine spun wool and linen and for the working class, homespun rough woollen cloth and linen.

Though most people managed to have leather shoes, for the very poor and beggars, footwear was made from wood or woven from rushes.

The middle class in Elizabethan times made much of family life. Upbringing was strict but loving and this seems to have been the case in the Shakespeare household.

We know that William must have been tough to succeed the way he did but he had another admirable trait: in later times his friend, the playwright Ben Johnson, described him as 'gentle' Shakespeare. Being tough and gentle are traits that are generally learned in the home and a tough but loving one at that.

It has been said that in Shakespeare's time children were viewed and treated as little adults. This is unlikely and childhood was almost certainly seen as a separate part of human development in most homes. The Elizabethans knew that children needed to be protected, cared for and loved. It seems obvious to us now, but they also became aware that a child's home life could affect the way they grow up.

With the exception of royalty and the aristocracy, a child was expected to work and girls could be married at the age of twelve and boys at fourteen. If parents died, the laws of the time did not allow anyone to inherit goods and property until they were twenty-one.

## Schooldays

The spread of creative ideas had come about in the period called the Renaissance which lasted from the 14th to the 16th century. The invention of printing and the availability of knowledge through books changed everything. Schools began to appear and those able to afford it sent their children to school; for the working classes it was hard work, poverty and ignorance as usual!

While still under the age of five it is likely that the young Shakespeare would have attended petty school – from the French *petit*, meaning 'small'. Girls also attended. They were sometimes called dame schools because they were run by an educated woman. Another name for the teacher was an 'abcedarius'.

Here William would have learned counting, the alphabet and basic reading and writing.

## ⊙-⊙ Fast Facts

### Shakespeare's alphabet!

The alphabet in Shakespeare's time had only twenty-four characters instead of our twenty-six. The letters 'j' and 'v' did not exist and were replaced by 'i' and 'u'. The letter 'y' could be seen replacing 'th' as in Ye Olde Inn. It was still pronounced 'The' and not 'Ye'. This was a leftover from Old English runes where the 'th' sound in the word 'the' was represented by the runic letter Þ called thorn. Early printers who came from the continent did not have this letter in their kit so chose to use the nearest which was a 'y'. Another common confusion is that the letter 's' often looks like an 'f'.

Counting, the alphabet and basic reading and writing were done from something called a hornbook – a small, wooden, paddle-shaped board on which was written numbers one to ten, the alphabet in capitals and lower case and the Lord's Prayer. This was covered in a thin, clear sheet of animal horn; hence the name, hornbook.

## ⌐o-o Fast Facts

### Can you believe it!

The horn of a cow grows yearly in rings similar to a tree. By placing the horn in hot water it grows soft and pliable and then a layer can be peeled off. Now it looks like a thin sheet of plastic and this was used to cover the hornbook.

As well as the hornbook, another tool in the Elizabethan classroom was a sheet of slate on which a pupil could write with chalk. The surface would then be wiped off with a damp cloth and re-used. This was because paper was hard to come by and therefore expensive, so it was used sparingly.

However, our young hero would also have learned how to make his own pen and ink.

The pen was made from a goose feather, also known as a quill. This was cut into a pen shape by a small sharp knife: a pen knife!

Ink was normally made from soot. All paper in those day was handmade, usually from old linen clothes which themselves had been made from a grass known as flax.

## Grammar school

It is a simple truth that school, on the whole, gives us the means to work in the modern world. School in Shakespeare's time was of a different order. The primary use of education was to mould children into becoming more religious through being able to read the Bible and other religious texts. Many people learned how to read but were not taught how to write. It doesn't work the other way, you cannot be taught to write without being able to read!

A grammar school education wasn't available to everyone: girls were excluded from schooling, except, as we have already said, in petty school, dame school or nursery. They were expected to learn all they needed from their mothers and husbands, though there were exceptions. For example, Queen Elizabeth I was a well-educated woman, although she was among a very tiny minority of women who enjoyed a good education.

Because his father held the post of bailiff, William was able to go to grammar school for free. In the case of Stratford, the grammar school was paid for by the Town Council so it was free to all boys anyway from the age of seven.

Only the middle classes or slightly better-off working classes would have sent their children to the grammar school. The rich employed private tutors while, as usual, the children of the poor stayed at home to work. In larger families, where there were enough hands to help with the daily chores, some working-class boys would have attended free schools.

William's father is thought to have been illiterate, although it is quite possible that he had basic reading skills but could not write. This does not mean he was not intelligent; just that he had not attended school, for in his day there was none to attend. There is a small clue on some family documents – the initial 'M' – that William's mother may have had writing skills.

In Shakespeare's time one hundred and sixty schools were set up in England, producing the most literate population in history. At the age of six or seven, William would have gone from petty school to a grammar school.

I say, 'would have', for we have no actual proof that William attended school, for there is no record. However, it is fairly obvious from his work that he had learned reading and writing and that he had studied Latin and was well-read in the great Latin writers and poets such as Ovid, Virgil and Horace.

The school that William would have attended from 1571, when he was seven years old, still exists in Stratford, is still in use and can be visited. It is now called the King Edward VI Grammar School but in Shakespeare's time it was called the King's New School. The masters were paid some £20 per year which, for the time, was a very high salary and this attracted the best teachers: two of its masters, Richard Fox and William Smyth, went on to found Corpus Christi College and Brasenose College at Oxford.

## Schoolwork

School then was quite different from nowadays. It began at six o' clock in the morning in summer and seven o' clock in winter:

> Then, the whining schoolboy, with his satchel
> And shining morning face, creeping like a snail
> Unwillingly to school.

IT'S NEARLY 6am.

School

Jacques in *As You Like It* Act 2, Scene 7

There was a break at eight for breakfast and another at midday for lunch. The day ended at six o' clock in the evening. There were no desks and the children sat on stools in petty school and benches in grammar school – it must have been pretty tiring with nothing to lean on!

From the age of seven through until young Will was ten, he would have been under the care of a teacher called an usher, a junior master who had probably just finished university. With the usher he would have learned grammar, logic, rhetoric, arithmetic, geometry, music and astronomy.

Although paper was not easy to come by schoolboys were still expected to keep what was called 'a commonplace book' in which to write unusual words, phrases, quotations, proverbs and the like for use in future essays.

Grammar was the most important subject, hence the term 'grammar school'. It was believed that true wisdom came from understanding the classical writers and they were best read in the original Latin and Greek.

Unlike nowadays when English is spoken the world over, the international language in Will's days was Latin. A young scholar was expected to learn all aspects of its grammar, know how to read and write the language and, most importantly, be able to speak it fluently. The textbook which was used in schools for another two hundred years was *Lily's Latin Grammar*.

## ☉̄ Fast Facts

### Thank you for the letter!

Another influential book of the time was by the great scholar Erasmus who had been born a hundred years earlier. His book *On Copiousness* taught students a hundred and fifty ways (synonyms) in Latin to say, 'Thank you for your letter.' Shakespeare seems to mock the book when, in *Love's Labour's Lost*, he has the schoolteacher, Holofernes, say:

' . . . ripe as the pomewater (*apple*), who now hangeth like a jewel in the ear of caelo, the sky, the welken, the heaven; and anon falleth like a crab (*apple*) on the face of terra, the soil, the land, the earth.'

Mock he might, but Shakespeare was not above playing with synonyms himself, as he has done above to comic effect!

There is an amusing piece in *The Merry Wives of Windsor* where Shakespeare seems to be remembering his schooldays. The characters are young William Page and Sir Hugh Evans, the schoolmaster. The piece is almost certainly referring to *Lily's Latin Grammar* which begins 'In nouns be two numbers, the singular and the plural. The singular number speaketh of one as *lapis*, a stone.'

Here is the piece:

**Evans:** What is *lapis*, William?

**William:** A stone.

**Evans:** And what is 'a stone' William?

**William:** A pebble.

**Evans:** No, it is *lapis*. I pray you, remember in your prain.  *brain*

**William:** *Lapis*.

**Evans:** That is good William.

From *The Merry Wives of Windsor* Act 4, Scene 1

The name Hugh Evans is Welsh and one of Shakespeare's schoolmasters, Thomas Jenkins, was Welsh. Shakespeare also calls the student, William – is this a coincidence or is the playwright revealing something of his past in the play?

Although in the exchange between William and Hugh Evans they are discussing Latin, the conversation is in English. But in young Will's time as soon as a pupil had a basic grasp of Latin he was expected to speak in nothing else but Latin.

To speak in English was punishable – not by detention but by birching!

Now, as fond fathers,
Having bound up the threatening twigs of birch,
Only to stick it in their children's sight
For terror, not to use, in time the rod
Becomes more mocked than feared; so our decrees,
Dead to infliction, to themselves are dead,
And Liberty plucks Justice by the nose,
The baby beats the nurse, and quite athwart
Goes all decorum.

The Duke in *Measure for Measure* Act 1, Scene 3

The origins of Shakespeare's name lie in old English and Anglo-Saxon. There have been many variations; for example his grandfather was referred to as Shakspere, Shakespeare, Shakkspere, Shaxpere and Shakstaff.

Nowadays people get upset when their names are spelled incorrectly. Not so in Shakespeare's time. This was because there was no set standard for how a word should be spelled. A name or even a word could be spelled three different ways on the same page!

A suggested meaning for the name goes back to a time when warriors used to shake their spears at the enemy. It was a fairly common name in the Midlands of England and the name Wagstaff may have similar origins.

Although there were no set standards in spelling, there were standards in handwriting. Basic handwriting would have been taught in petty school. Once at grammar school the job of teaching handwriting was done by a scrivener (from the Latin *scribere* meaning 'to write'). Shakespeare wrote in what is referred to as a 'secretary' or 'secretarial hand'.

Secretary hand was probably taken from a handwriting book by Beau Chesne published in 1570. It also had set forms of abbreviation to assist the speed at which the writer could note down what was being said – important if someone is dictating a letter to you in a hurry!

*So you think this is perfect?*

Nowadays secretaries are usually women; but in Elizabethan times they were all men. The other form of writing was the 'court hand'. This was especially beautiful with additional curls and lines and was more orderly and refined.

Absolutely Perfect

DRAT!

Another school subject mentioned previously is rhetoric. Nowadays rhetoric is often used to mean pretentious language but its main definition is 'the art and study of using language effectively to influence others'. Shakespeare was good at this or at the very least he had a good ear for it. His plays contain many moments of high rhetoric as in, for example, the following speech by Shylock from the play *The Merchant of Venice*, Act 3, Scene 1.

> I am a Jew. Hath not a Jew eyes? Hath not a Jew hands, organs, dimensions, senses, affections, passions? fed with the same food, hurt with the same weapons, subject to the same diseases, healed by the same means, warmed and cooled by the same winter and summer as a Christian is? — if you prick us, do we not bleed? if you tickle us, do we not laugh? if you poison us, do we not die? and if you wrong us, shall we not revenge?

As already stated, the major reason why schools were set up by Elizabeth I in the first place was so that people would be able to read the Bible and be more religious in their outlook – and by religious, she meant Protestant and not Catholic. In time, children would read the entire Bible and be able to quote long passages from memory. Children were also taught to memorise long passages of Latin and Greek writing. Take this book as an example: it would not be unusual for children to be able to stand up and recite three pages of this text from memory!

If this seems amazing, think how many different things you are learning at the one time. Young Will and his fellow pupils worked on only a very few subjects. If you think school is boring, think yourself lucky. If you could travel through time and found yourself sitting beside

Will, you would go completely bonkers in a week!

But there was a great advantage for Will in learning this way: he was later able to form great chunks of stage-plays in his head, work out the way he wanted to say things and then be able to write it all down without having to go back and correct anything. This was very handy when a sheet of paper was so expensive!

Will's friend, the playwright Ben Jonson, famously said that while he admired the fact that Will could write pages and pages of a play with little or no correction, it might have been better if he had – meaning that he thought some of the writing was bad and should have been revised or corrected! But we need to remember that although Will was Jonson's friend, they were both in direct competition with each other as playwrights!

At about the age of nine or ten, William would have come under the care of the schoolmaster, Simon Hunt. By this time, his grasp of Latin would probably be better than that of a university graduate in the language today. He would have been reading the great Roman writers like Seneca, Horace and Ovid in their own language.

It was Ovid, born Publius Ovidius Naso in Sulmo, Italy in 43 BC, and his great narrative poem, *Metamorphosis*, that would come to dominate Shakespeare's artistic mind. *Metamorphosis* is a retelling of many of the ancient Greek and Roman myths. Many of the characters that appear in Ovid's *Metamorphosis* find their way into Shakespeare's plays. In particular, it was the 1567 translation of the poem by Arthur Golding that is said to have been Shakespeare's most treasured book.

PLEASE WILL, JUST A LITTLE LOOK AT YOUR BOOK?

MINE ... MINE, ALL MINE!

Presumably Young Shakespeare showed promise as a student of literature and it is likely, if this was so, that his reasonably wealthy parents or his schoolmasters provided him with books to read. If his parents were indeed illiterate he would have been expected to read to them and his brothers and sisters.

There is much in his plays to suggest that his knowledge of the world was well above average. Perhaps his tutors, who would have had their own library, also provided him with books to read.

## Home life

As a middle-class boy Young Will would have been expected to have good manners at home. Below is part of a poem by Francis Seager in the *School of Virtue and Book of Good Nurture* (1557) that was popular at the time:

> For rudeness it is thy potage to sup
> Or speak to any, his head in the cup.
> Thy knife so be sharp to cut fair thy meat;
> Thy mouth not too full when thou dost eat;
> Not smacking thy lips, As commonly do hogs,
> Nor gnawing the bones, As if were dogs;

NOW GNAW AT YOUR BONE *ELEGANTLY*, WILL.

NO DOGS ALLOWED AT THE TABLE, YOUNG MAN.

Such rudeness abhor, Such beastliness fly,
At the table behave thy self mannerly . . .
Pick not thy teeth at the table sitting,
Nor use at thy meat over much spitting;
This rudness of youth is to be abhorred;
Thyself mannerly behave at the board.

As said before, it is likely that Will had a strict but loving home life. Because of his father's position as mayor of Stratford he would have had certain privileges. This did not mean he would have had it easy. Will was a hard worker as a man and this he must have learned as a boy working beside his father.

Part of the house was used for his father John's trade which involved buying skins, curing or tanning them and then cutting them into gloves, belts, purses and other small but desirable leather goods. Materials such as dog excrement and human urine were used in the process of preparing leather so there must have been a few disagreeable aromas around the house – people were paid to supply urine and a bucket was available at the door for this purpose. Instead of spending a penny, you were paid one!

Tanning pits, probably used by John Shakespeare and others, were recently discovered off Henley Street, close by the Birthplace (see page 122). In the pits, leathers were left to soak in certain chemicals. This was to prevent the leather rotting, to colour it and in some cases to make it waterproof.

Gloves were in great fashion and people paid good money for them. Only the finest leather was used and it was often perfumed and embroidered with silver and gold thread. It is shocking to us now but one of the most commonly used leathers was the skin of a dog. One week the dog would be sitting on your lap, the next you could be wearing it!

## ᴏᴏ Fast Facts

### Urine, flour and eggs!

The preparation of skins for gloves was a lengthy and complicated process. In brief, it involved treating the skin with lime to loosen the hair. This was scraped off and any flesh scraped from the inside. The next step was to soak it in a solution of dog excrement or urine which softened the leather. Next it was soaked in a bran solution which formed lactic acid and neutralised the lime. When the skin floated to the surface it was then ready for a last scrape before tanning. Tanning is where the skin is treated and becomes leather with tannin obtained from boiled oak bark. After this it was treated with alum (aluminium salts), then flour and egg yolks before being worked in a variety of ways to make it dry, soft and ready for cutting.

The town of Stratford would have had workshops for almost every trade imaginable: as well as glovers, there were shoemakers, ropemakers, spinners who made yarn and thread, weavers who made cloth, tailors who made clothes, furniture-makers, pewterers who made plates and drinking vessels, builders, blacksmiths and carpenters. During his childhood years, Young Will would come into contact with all of them and learn a little of their skills – a useful education for a writer.

Will's family was fairly wealthy for a time. John Shakespeare bought another property in Greenhill Street as well as working his father's land at nearby Snitterfield. It would seem that the young Shakespeare could look forward to a privileged life. We can guess that he was certainly well cared for.

His father was a successful businessman, who must have employed people in his trade and who must also have travelled a lot. This would mean that his mother Mary would have known the business as well and been able to run things while John was away. From this we can guess that Will probably had a nanny. It is unlikely that she would have been able to read but, as was common among nannies of long ago, she would have had a fund of folktales to amuse the children in her care.

As books were scarce and the oral tradition still strong, his mother would almost certainly have added her fair share of stories. We can see from the works of William Shakespeare that he had a great knowledge of folklore. Was this where all his great plays, poems and songs started?

William Shakespeare also shows a great knowledge of wildlife and his plays are full of references to birds and flowers, many of which he would have seen in and around Stratford. And there are many, such as the ostrich, pelican or vulture, that he would have found in books or seen brought in as curios by sailors.

Flowers he would have known include cowslip, daffodil, daisy, dog-rose, lady-smock, lily, marigold, pansy, primrose, rose and violet.

Birds he would have known include the blackbird (ousel-cock), bunting, chough, cock, cormorant, crow, cuckoo, dove, duck, eagle, falcon, finch, fowl, goose, guinea hen, hedge sparrow, heron, jay, kestrel, kingfisher, kite, lapwing, lark, loon, magpie, mallard, martin (martlet) nightingale, osprey, ostrich, owl, parrot, partridge, peacock, pelican, pheasant, phoenix, pigeon, quail, raven, rook, sea gull, sparrow, starling, swallow, swan, thrush, turkey, vulture, woodcock, and wren.

## Games

Assuming that William, like all children, enjoyed playing games, this would have been almost exclusively with children from his own middle-class background – working-class children would have been working. Some of the games he would have played are summed up in a poem from that time:

> To wrestle, play at stooleballe, or to runne,
> To pitch the barre, or to shoote off a gunne,
> To play at loggats, Nine-holes, or Ten-pinnes,
> To try it out at football by the shinnes.

Stoolball was a bit like cricket, pitch the bar like tossing the caber and loggats like throwing the horseshoe. Other popular games and sports were wrestling, skittles, hopscotch, ninepins (bowling), blind-man's-buff and swimming in the River Avon – a pig's bladder was often used as a float!

Popular sports that would shock most people today were various forms of baiting where animals were set against each other, including dog against dog in dog-baiting, dog or bull against bull in bull-baiting, and dog or bear against bear in bear-baiting.

Baiting was common in London and it's suggested that the reason the Globe and other theatres of the time were shaped the way they were (in a circle open to the elements with galleries all the way round and a yard for standing spectators in the middle) was because they were originally used to watch such sports.

When William was four, John Shakespeare became town bailiff or mayor. This would have pushed the family to the forefront of all that went on in Stratford. Before his father was made town bailiff, Will would have seen travelling plays being performed in the street and these would certainly have left a great impression on the Young Shakespeare.

When William's father became bailiff one of his jobs was to vet these plays. In other words, John Shakespeare had to check if a play was suitable for performance in public. This would mean viewing a private performance in which Will would be able to see close-at-hand all the actions of the play and to meet the players.

KILL, KILL, KILL THE BADDIE.

Who can doubt that such an event would have had a profound effect on a small boy? In later life, William joined just such a group travelling the country and ended up in London.

# Religion

As with everyone else during the Elizabethan era, religion dominated the life of Young Will Shakespeare. Heaven, the home of God and His angels, was (and still is for many) a real place where the good would live for eternity in bliss. Hell, the home of Satan and his demons, was also a real place – an all-too-real place to many – where sinners were condemned to eternal torture in fire and brimstone. The thought of ending-up there after death understandably terrified people.

Shakespeare's family were outwardly Protestant but there is some evidence to suggest that they had Catholic sympathies. Apart from a brief period during the reign of Queen Mary (Bloody Mary), England had been a Protestant country since the times of Henry VIII. Elizabeth I had for years steered a middle path that kept Catholic and Protestant at bay.

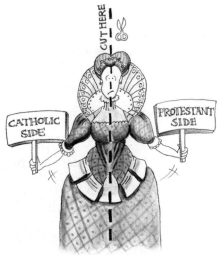

In 1570 the Pope declared Elizabeth I's reign illegitimate which angered many Protestants and resulted in Catholics being persecuted. Practising Catholicism became a crime and those guilty of it were also guilty of treason – for it was assumed that they wanted a Catholic king or queen – and the punishment for treason was death.

A priest with a connection to Shakespeare, Father Edmund Campion, was hung, drawn and quartered for spreading Catholic ideas. Cruel torture and being put to death in the name of religion were fairly commonplace in Shakespeare's time, which explains the fact that there is both cruelty and violent death in his plays – and to think that Jesus proclaimed peace and love!

## The lost years

In the years before leaving for fame and fortune in London, Young William would have left school at the age of fourteen but not gone on to university – possibly because of his father's growing financial difficulties at this time. It is likely he joined his father in the gloving trade. At the age of eighteen, he married Anne Hathaway and became a father.

Of these things, we have some knowledge and the rest we can only guess. One possibility is that he became a teacher and worked for a wealthy family near Lancaster. Unless some as yet unknown proof turns up, these times in Will's life

will always be referred to as the 'lost years'.

What we can be certain of is that he became, in his lifetime, a famous and successful playwright and actor who performed before Elizabeth I and James VI of Scotland (who was also James I of England). Since then he has come to be regarded as perhaps the greatest writer of all time.

What made him so great? The clues to a person's success can often be found in their childhood. Perhaps from what you have read so far about the Young Shakespeare you might get some ideas. This we do know – and I'm sorry to have to tell you – his success mainly comes down to ambition and hard work!

# SHAKESPEARE'S WORKS

## Words and Shakespeare

The English language now has about one and a half to two million words, if technical words and terms are added. In Shakespeare's time there would have been less than 150,000 words. The average person today has a vocabulary of 10,000 to 20,000 words with an active vocabulary of 5,000. In other words, the total number of words that they commonly use in their own speech and writing is 5,000.

Shakespeare's complete works use a total of 884,647 words and 29,066 different words. Some of these words may have already been in use and Shakespeare was the first to record them, but we know that he (and many other writers) did coin (create) new words, and due to the popularity of his work they are now part of our everyday language.

Words created by William Shakespeare include the following:

accused, addiction, amazement, arouse, assassinate, blushing, champion, circumstantial, compromise, courtship, countless, critic, dawn, epileptic, elbow, excitement, exposure, frugal, generous, gossip, hint, impartial, invulnerable, jaded, label, lonely, luggage, majestic, negotiate, obscene, premeditated, puke, scuffle, torture, tranquil, varied and worthless.

Below is a list of the most commonly used words in Shakespeare:

the, and, I, to, of, a, you, my, that, in.

Compare this to the most commonly used words in English nowadays:

the, of, and, a, to, in, is, you, that, it.

Notice the presence of 'I' and 'my' in Shakespeare's list which in our everyday language are usually about 20th and 80th in a list of the 100 most commonly used English words. Can you explain this?

(The answer: in the plays the characters often talk about themselves, their feelings or possessions. In real life we tend not to be so self-centred.)

# Everyday expressions

Many of the everyday expressions we use go back to Shakespeare. Here are a few from his plays (and there are many more!):

As white as driven snow  *(A Winter's Tale)*

Dead as a doornail  *(King Henry VI)*

Fool's paradise  *(Romeo and Juliet)*

I have not slept one wink  *(Cymbeline)*

Into thin air  *(The Tempest)*

More fool you  *(The Taming of the Shrew)*

My own flesh and blood  *(The Merchant of Venice)*

The be-all and end-all  *(Macbeth)*

Though this be madness, yet there is method in't  *(Hamlet)*

Throw cold water on it  *(The Merry Wives of Windsor)*

Wear my heart on my sleeve  *(Othello)*

Neither a borrower nor a lender be  *(Hamlet)*

. . . to thine own self be true  *(Hamlet)*

. . . it was Greek to me  *(Julius Caesar)*

The course of true love never did run smooth. *(A Midsummer Night's Dream)*

In my mind's eye  *(Hamlet)*

Parting is such sweet sorrow *(Romeo and Juliet)*
I am a man more sinned against than sinning
*(King Lear)*
'Tis neither here nor there *(Othello)*
But love is blind *(The Merchant of Venice)*

# Puns

Shakespeare is often criticised because of his frequent use of puns, many of which would have made the literate groan; but we have to remember he was playing to a varied audience who were often not literate and who would have revelled in the word play. The extract that follows is from *King Henry IV*, Part One, Act 2, Scene 4:

**Poins:**

Come, your reason, Jack, your reason.

**Falstaff:**

What, upon compulsion? Zounds, and I were at the strappado or all the racks in the world, I would not tell you upon compulsion. Give you a reason on compulsion? If reasons were as plentiful as blackberries, I would give no man a reason upon compulsion, I.

This extract from includes a pun on the word 'reason' and relies on us knowing how words from the time were pronounced. In the time of Shakespeare, the word 'reason' was pronounced 'raisin' and raisins were a luxury – and not nearly as plentiful as blackberries! 'Upon compulsion' means being forced or compelled to give a reason. 'Zounds' was a contraction of 'God's wounds' and a mild form of swearing. 'Strappado' is a torture machine. Here arc a few more examples of puns.

From *Romeo and Juliet*, Act 1, Scene 4:

**Romeo:**

Give me a torch: I am not for this ambling.
Being but heavy, I will bear the **light**.

A play on the word 'light' as opposed to heavy and meaning the torch.

**Mercutio:**

Nay, gentle Romeo, we must have you dance.

**Romeo:**

Not I, believe me. You have dancing shoes
With nimble **soles**, I have a **soul** of lead
So stakes me to the ground I cannot move.

A play on the words 'sole' and 'soul'.

**Mercutio:**

You are a lover. Borrow Cupid's wings,

And **soar** with them above a common bound.

**Romeo:**

I am too **sore** enpierced with his shaft

To **soar** with his light feathers, and so bound

I cannot bound a pitch above dull woe.

Under love's heavy burden do I sink.

A play on the words 'soar' and 'sore'.

*A little later*

**Mercutio:**

That dreamers often **lie**.

**Romeo:**

In bed asleep, while they do dream things true.

A play on the word 'lie' meaning to fib and to be on one's back.

From *King Richard III*, Act 1, Scene 1:

**Richard, Duke of Gloucester:**
Now is the winter of our discontent
Made glorious summer by this **son** of York;

If you didn't get it, the pun here is that winter is made summer because of the 'son' (i.e. 'sun') – a play on the words 'son' and 'sun'.

# Insults

Some of the words of insult used by Shakespeare include:

beslubbering, gorbellied, bat-fowling, beef-witted, beetle-headed, clay-brained, fen-sucked, guts-griping, swag-bellied, clack-dish, clotpole, hugger mugger, maggot pie, moldwarp, puttock

String three together and you have a superior class of insult! For example:

You beslubbering, clay-brained maggot-pie!

Not that it is admirable to insult anyone, but the insults of today pale in comparison to the insults of Elizabethan times and particularly those featured in Shakespeare's plays! Here are a few examples:

An ass head and a coxcomb and a knave, a thin-faced knave and gull.

From *Twelfth Night*

A foul and pestilent congregation of vapours. What a piece of work is man!

From *Hamlet*

Out of my door, you witch, you hag, you baggage, you polecat, you ronyon (scabby beast).

From *The Merry Wives of Windsor*

Scurvy, old, filthy, scurry lord.

From *All's Well That Ends Well*

Thou art a boil, a plague sore, an embossed carbuncle in my corrupted blood.

From *King Lear*

---

## ᴏᴏ Fast Facts

### Insult or compliment?

'What lovely teeth you have!' Because of the arrival of sugar from plantations in the West Indies it was common for people to have blackened teeth; so much so that people often blackened their teeth cosmetically to get the same effect!

HOW BLACK, MY LADY?

# Shakespeare and the movies

The works of Shakespeare have been filmed more times than those of any other playwright, yet he died two hundred years before film was invented! The first film was in 1899 when Herbert Beerbohm Tree performed short excerpts from *King John*; the film lasted all of four minutes! By 1929 over two hundred silent films had been made from Shakespeare's plays. It seems a little strange now to think of a silent Shakespearean production considering his plays are so wordy! Since 1930, and if you include television, there have been over two hundred films. Add radio plays to this and the number of productions worldwide is almost certainly in the thousands.

## ᴏᴏ Fast Facts

### He or she?

Although in the film *Shakespeare in Love* Viola DeLessops (Gwyneth Paltrow) plays Juliet in their production of *Romeo and Juliet*, the first woman to actually play on stage and in a Shakespeare play was Margaret Hughes in 1660: she played the part of Desdemona in *Othello*. Before that, female roles were always played by boys!

# Shakespeare's tragedies

The word tragedy is from the Greek words *tragos* meaning goat and *oide* meaning song, hence 'goat song' – a strange name indeed!

It comes from the ancient Greek plays when the story was carried along by what we now call the chorus or background singers. In ancient times they dressed in goatskins hence the name 'goat song'.

Among Shakespeare's plays, the tragedies are considered his greater works, including *Hamlet, Julius Caesar, Macbeth, Othello and King Lear*. They contain the highest drama and deal with issues that are deeply affecting such as family relations, power struggles, obsessions and betrayals.

The death and destruction that we meet in Shakespeare's tragedies are things that we all want to avoid and should they visit us, which in time they might and will, they can have a great effect on our lives.

# Shakespeare's villains

What made Shakespeare different from other playwrights and one of the reasons why his plays are still relevant today is that he gives a voice to everyone. Even his villains, with perhaps the exception of Iago in *Othello*, are well rounded and very human. Prior to Shakespeare (and since) villains were shown to be completely evil and inhuman.

We still talk about atrocities such as the Nazi holocaust or the genocide in Rwanda as being inhuman. They were not; they were carried out by humans who were capable of being loving and kind on the one hand and ruthless killers on the other.

OH NO, I'M A GOODIE AND A BADDIE!

What makes Shakespeare so great is not just the beauty and richness of his language and the wonderful structure of plot and play; it is the fact that he saw the best and the worst in his characters. Put simply: it wasn't just a case of 'we are the good guys and they are the bad guys'; as in the real world there is good and bad in all of us and that is what puts real humanity into his plays.

# Shakespeare's comedies

Unfortunately some of the humour in Shakespeare's plays is lost to us. Sometimes it is because our sense of humour has changed over the centuries and sometimes it is because changes in our language mean that we miss many of his puns or play on words.

This aside, Shakespeare is still wonderfully funny. Many of his jokes are typical schoolboy jokes that are still with us. For example, in the following line from *King Lear*:

'Blow, winds, and crack your cheeks.'

he would mean the cheeks of those little wind cherubs you see on old maps but at the same time he would also mean the cheeks of your bottom!

## Shakespeare's sonnets

In all, Shakespeare wrote one hundred and fifty-four sonnets. They were private, and were published, as far as we know, without Shakespeare's approval in 1609.

The word 'sonnet' is from the Italian *sonetto*, meaning a 'little song', and this verse form was developed in the 13th century by the Italian poet, Petrarch.

Originally sonnets were love poems and consisted of fourteen lines – an opening eight lines (octet) and a closing six lines (sextet).

The rhyme scheme was:

**a b b a a b b a** and **c d e c d e**.

In other words, lines one and four rhymed and two and three rhymed, and so on.

In Shakespeare's sonnets you still have the octet and sextet but there is a different rhyme scheme:

**a b a b c d c d** and **e f e f g g**.

With the exception of Sonnet 145 they are all written in iambic pentameter.

# ⊙⊙ Fast Facts

## Iambic pentameter

Many of Shakespeare's plays and poems were set out in a rhythmical form called iambic pentameter. An iamb is an ancient rhythmical form which is simply stated as da/**DUM** – the stress is on the second syllable, e.g. Shake/**SPEARE**. Pentameter means a measure of five. Put simply, there are five iambs per line as in:

Shall **I** com**PARE** thee **TO** a **SUM**mer's **DAY**?

The opposite of an iamb is a troche and a trochaic rhythm runs **DA**/dum.

## *Sonnet 18*

This is probably Shakespeare's most famous sonnet. In it he is saying that a summer's day can be too rough, too hot or too short whereas his dear friend is warm, gentle and has an everlasting beauty. He ends by saying that this beauty will never fade but will live on forever in the lines of his sonnet, which people will read down through the many years to come.

Shall I compare thee to a summer's day?
Thou art more lovely and more temperate:
Rough winds do shake the darling buds of May,
And summer's lease hath all too short a date:
Sometime too hot the eye of heaven shines,
And often is his gold complexion dimmed,
And every fair from fair sometime declines,
By chance, or nature's changing course, untrimmed:
But thy eternal summer shall not fade,
Nor lose possession of that fair thou ow'st,
Nor shall death brag thou wander'st in his shade,
When in eternal lines to time thou grow'st,
So long as men can breathe, or eyes can see,
So long lives this, and this gives life to thee.

## Sonnet 116

In this sonnet, Shakespeare is referring to love in its deepest sense. He shows how much he admires true love that is constant and strong and enduring. He says that if he is wrong about the nature of true love, then he will take back all his writings on love.

Let me not to the marriage of true minds
Admit impediments. Love is not love
Which alters when it alteration finds,
Or bends with the remover to remove:
O, no, it is an ever-fixed mark,
That looks on tempests and is never shaken;
It is the star to every wand'ring bark,          *ship*
Whose worth's unknown, although his height
be taken.
Love's not Time's fool, though rosy lips and
cheeks
Within his bending sickle's compass come;
Love alters not with his brief hours and
weeks,
But bears it out even to the edge of doom.
If this be error and upon me proved,
I never writ, nor no man ever loved.

## Sonnet 130

In this sonnet, Shakespeare is making a dig at other writers of sonnets who describe their lovers as being like angels or immortal beings. He is making fun of the use of such metaphors and similies.

Let's face it, if your love had hair of golden thread, cheeks like rose petals and breasts like snow you'd think she was dressed up for 'Trick or Treat'!

Shakespeare ends by saying he loves her all the more because of her ordinary beauty and plainness. Nice one Will!

My mistress' eyes are nothing like the sun;
Coral is far more red, than her lips red;
If snow be white, why then her breasts are
dun;

If hairs be wires, black wires grow on her head.
I have seen roses damasked, red and white,
But no such roses see I in her cheeks;
And in some perfumes is there more delight
Than in the breath that from my mistress reeks.
I love to hear her speak, yet well I know
That music hath a far more pleasing sound:
I grant I never saw a goddess go;
My mistress, when she walks, treads on the ground:
And yet by heaven, I think my love as rare
As any she belied with false compare.

## ◦◌ Fast Facts

### Black wires and golden threads

'Wires' in Shakespeare's time did not have the industrial meaning they do nowadays but would have referred to the finely spun gold threads woven into the fancy hairdos of the time, so its use would have been more poetic!

## Sonnet 145

This is far from being Shakespeare's best sonnet and is thought by some to have been written when he was a young man.

What makes it interesting is that some think it refers to Anne Hathaway in a punning sort of way, i.e. 'hate away' really means 'Hathaway' and that 'And save my life' really is 'Anne saved my life'. It is a strange piece and may just mean that even the best of writers have bad days!

Those lips that Love's own hand did make,
Breathed forth the sound that said 'I hate',
To me that languished for her sake;
But when she saw my woeful state,
Straight in her heart did mercy come,
Chiding that tongue that, ever sweet,
Was used in giving gentle doom,
And taught it thus anew to greet:
'I hate' she altered with an end
That followed it as gentle day
Doth follow night, who like a fiend
From heaven to hell is flown away.
'I hate', from 'hate' away she threw,
And saved my life, saying 'not you'.

# Shakespeare's songs

During Shakespeare's times, music played an important part in people's everyday lives just as it does today.

There are more than a hundred songs in Shakespeare's works and while they might not be included among today's top hits they were no doubt much enjoyed at the time!

Having said that, both Elvis Costello and Sting have recorded songs by Shakespeare and many classical and folk artists still sing and record his songs.

When that I was and a little tiny boy,
With hey, ho, the wind and the rain,
A foolish thing was but a toy,
For the rain it raineth every day.

But when I came to man's estate,
With hey, ho, the wind and the rain,
'Gainst knaves and thieves men shut their gate,
For the rain it raineth every day.

The clown in *Twelfth Night*, Act 5, Scene 1

Full fathom five thy father lies,     *6 feet x 5 = 30 feet*
Of his bones are coral made;
Those are pearls that were his eyes,
Nothing of him that doth fade
But doth suffer a sea-change
Into something rich and strange.
Sea-nymphs hourly ring his knell.
Ding-dong.
Hark! now I hear them,
Ding-dong, bell.

Ariel in *The Tempest*, Act 1, Scene 2

Under the greenwood tree
Who loves to lie with me,
And turn his merry note
Unto the sweet bird's throat,
Come hither, come hither, come hither.
Here shall he see
No enemy,
But winter and rough weather.

Amiens in *As You Like It*, Act 2, Scene 5

When icicles hang by the wall
And Dick the shepherd, blows his nail
And Tom bears logs into the hall
And milk comes frozen home in pail,
When blood is nipped and ways be foul,
Then nightly sings the staring owl:
Tu-whit, Tu-whoo! A merry note,
While greasy Joan doth keel the pot.      *cool by stirring*

When all aloud the wind doth blow
And coughing drowns the parson's saw
And birds sit brooding in the snow
And Marion's nose looks red and raw,
When roasted crabs hiss in the bowl,
Then nightly sings the staring owl,
Tu-whit, Tu-whoo! A merry note,
While greasy Joan doth keel the pot.

Hiems in *Love's Labour's Lost*, Act 5, Scene 2

# Extracts from the plays of Shakespeare

## *As You Like It*

This play revolves round Rosalind, daughter of Duke Senior. The Duke has been banished to the Forest of Arden by his brother Duke Frederick but Rosalind has remained at court. When she herself is banished she disguises herself as a young man named Ganymede and leaves with Frederick's daughter Celia disguised as his sister Aliena.

The other players are the brothers Orlando, Oliver and Jacques deBoys. Orlando has been mistreated by Oliver and also finds himself in the Forest but not before falling in love with Rosalind. In the forest he meets Ganymede and declares his love for Rosalind, not seeing through the disguise; in time she falls for him. In the end everyone makes up and, presumably, lives happily ever after!

Part of the fun of the play would be the fact that in Shakespeare's time a boy would play the part of Rosalind playing a boy, Ganymede!

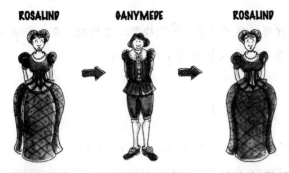

ROSALIND     GANYMEDE     ROSALIND

**BOY DRESSED UP AS ROSALIND, A GIRL**     **BOY ACTING AS ROSALIND NOW DISGUISED AS – YOU'VE GUESSED IT – A BOY**     **BACK TO BOY DRESSED UP AS ROSALIND, A GIRL**

The following passage from Act 2, Scene 7 of *As You Like It* is spoken by Jaques, one of the lords attending Duke Senior, in which he looks at the seven ages of man.

**Jaques:**

> All the world's a stage,
> And all the men and women merely players.
> They have their exits and their entrances,
> And one man in his time plays many parts,
> His acts being seven ages. At first the infant,
> Mewling and puking in the nurse's arms.
> And then the whining school-boy, with his satchel
> And shining morning face, creeping like snail
> Unwillingly to school. And then the lover,
> Sighing like furnace, with a woeful ballad
> Made to his mistress' eyebrow. Then a soldier,

Full of strange oaths and bearded like the pard, *panther*

Jealous in honour, sudden and quick in quarrel,

Seeking the bubble reputation

Even in the cannon's mouth. And then the justice,

In fair round belly with good capon lined, *with a large stomach filled with good chicken meat*

With eyes severe and beard of formal cut,

Full of wise saws, and modern instances,

And so he plays his part. The sixth age shifts

Into the lean and slippered pantaloon,

With spectacles on nose and pouch on side,

His youthful hose, well sav'd, a world too wide

For his shrunk shank, and his big manly voice,

Turning again toward childish treble, pipes

And whistles in his sound. Last scene of all,

That ends this strange eventful history,

Is second childishness and mere oblivion,

Sans teeth, sans eyes, sans taste, sans everything.

## Hamlet, Prince of Denmark

*Hamlet* is accepted as Shakespeare's masterpiece. It is also his longest play – the most recent film version is over four hours long.

Hamlet meets the ghost of his father who reveals that the new king of Denmark had him poisoned – the new king also happens to be both Hamlet's uncle, Claudius, and his new stepfather.

To try and find out the truth, Hamlet pretends to be mad and, with the aid of a group of travelling players, he puts on a play based on the alleged murder of his father (a play within a play). Claudius's reaction to Hamlet's play convinces Hamlet that his father was indeed poisoned by his uncle.

Will Hamlet take his revenge? In the end most of the cast meet their end, including Hamlet.

In the passage that follows from Act 3, Scene 1, Hamlet is musing about the fact that although he is unhappy with his life, which is full of torments, he is unsure and nervous about what death might bring. In other words, 'Life is bad but death might be even worse!'

**Hamlet:**

To be, or not to be, that is the question:
Whether 'tis nobler in the mind to suffer
The slings and arrows of outrageous fortune,
Or to take arms against a sea of troubles
And by opposing end them? To die – to sleep,
No more; and by a sleep to say we end
The heart-ache and the thousand natural shocks
That flesh is heir to: 'tis a consummation
Devoutly to be wish'd. To die, to sleep;
To sleep, perchance to dream – ay, there's the rub: *difficulty*
For in that sleep of death what dreams may come,
When we have shuffled off this mortal coil, *bustle of life*
Must give us pause – there's the respect
That makes calamity of so long life.
For who would bear the whips and scorns of time, *insults*
The oppressor's wrong, the proud man's contumely, *insulting treatment*
The pangs of disprized love, the law's delay,
The insolence of office, and the spurns
That patient merit of the unworthy takes,
When he himself might his quietus make *death*
*large needle* With a bare bodkin? Who would fardels bear, *burdens*
To grunt and sweat under a weary life,
But that the dread of something after death,
The undiscovered country from whose bourn

No traveller returns, puzzles the will,
And makes us rather bear those ills we have
Than fly to others that we know not of?
Thus conscience does make cowards of us all,
And thus the native hue of resolution
Is sicklied o'er with the pale cast of thought,
And enterprises of great pitch and moment
With this regard their currents turn awry          *aside*
And lose the name of action. Soft you now,
The fair Ophelia! Nymph, in thy orisons           *prayers*
Be all my sins remember'd.

## 👓 Fast Facts

### Who's the best?

The role of Hamlet is a demanding and difficult one as he is a complicated person with many different sides to his character. It is also the longest part in any Shakespeare play, with 1,507 lines to learn.

Many famous actors have played Hamlet, with David Tennant (recently Dr Who in the TV series) being one of them. John Gielgud (from 1930) and Laurence Olivier (1948 film) are regarded as the greatest Hamlets of the earlier part of the 20th century while Mark Rylance (2000) and Simon Russell-Beale (2000) are admired by many for their performances in the 21st century. More than fifty women have played Hamlet, including Sarah Bernhardt (from 1899) and Angela Winkler (2000).

## *Julius Caesar*

When Julius Caesar returns to Rome after defeating the Celts of Gaul, members of the Senate (the council that rules Rome) fear that the republic will disappear and a dictatorship under Caesar as king will take over.

To prevent this, they plot Caesar's murder. Because Caesar has been so popular they convince one of his friends, Marcus Brutus, to lead the plotters and turn the people against Caesar. On the Ides of March (15 March), Brutus and the assassins stab Caesar to death in the Senate building.

SURPRISE!
I'M WITH *THEM*
NOW, JULIUS.

The extract that follows from Act 3, Scene 2, contains some of Shakespeare's most best-known lines. In this clever speech, Mark Antony speaks in praise of Caesar and manages to turn the people against the plotters and in particular Brutus, who has just claimed that the murder of Caesar had been done in the name of freedom.

**Mark Antony:**

Friends, Romans, countrymen, lend me your ears:

I come to bury Caesar, not to praise him.

The evil that men do lives after them:

The good is oft interred with their bones.

So let it be with Caesar. The noble Brutus

Hath told you Caesar was ambitious:

If it were so, it was a grievous fault,

And grievously hath Caesar answered it.

Here, under leave of Brutus and the rest

(For Brutus is an honourable man;

So are they all, all honourable men)

Come I to speak in Caesar's funeral.

He was my friend, faithful and just to me;

But Brutus says, he was ambitious,

And Brutus is an honourable man.

He hath brought many captives home to Rome,

Whose ransoms did the general coffers fill.
Did this in Caesar seem ambitious?
When that the poor have cried, Caesar hath
wept:
Ambition should be made of sterner stuff.
Yet Brutus says, he was ambitious,
And Brutus is an honourable man.
You all did see, that on the Lupercal*
I thrice presented him a kingly crown,
Which he did thrice refuse. Was this
ambition?
Yet Brutus says, he was ambitious,
And sure he is an honourable man.
I speak not to disprove what Brutus spoke,
But here I am to speak what I do know.
You all did love him once, not without cause:
What cause withholds you then to mourn for
him?
O judgment, thou art fled to brutish beasts
And men have lost their reason. Bear with me.
My heart is in the coffin there with Caesar,
And I must pause till it come back to me.

*A festival on 15 February to the god  Lupercus – a god like Pan.

## *Macbeth*

Because of a theatrical superstition worldwide that any company performing this play will have horrible luck, the play is often referred to as the 'Scottish play' rather than *Macbeth*.

The real Macbeth took the throne of Scotland in 1040, after killing his cousin, King Duncan I, in a battle near Elgin in the Moray district of Scotland.

According to Shakespeare, Macbeth meets three witches who prophesy, among other things, that one day he will be king of Scotland. When King Duncan visits him, Macbeth, urged on by his wife, murders the king. He lays the blame on others and is crowned king.

In the end, he is defeated by another Scottish lord, MacDuff, who restores Duncan's son Malcolm to the throne.

The three witches or Weird Sisters are based on the three Norns of Norse or Viking mythology. The Norns  represent the past, the present and the future (as do the Weird Sisters and the three Fates of Greek mythology).

We can also tell from the witches brew in the extract below that Shakespeare had actual knowledge of witchcraft,  and he was certainly a wizard with words!

**First Witch:**
Thrice the brinded cat hath mewed.    *brindled/striped*

**Second Witch:**
Thrice and once the hedge-pig whined.    *hedgehog*

**Third Witch:**
Harpier cries 'Tis time, 'tis time.    *harpy/female demon*

**First Witch:**
Round about the cauldron go;
In the poisoned entrails throw.
Toad, that under cold stone
Days and nights has thirty-one
Sweltered venom, sleeping got,
Boil thou first in the charmed pot.

**All:**
Double, double toil and trouble:
Fire burn; and cauldron bubble.

### Second Witch:

Fillet of a fenny snake,       *swampy*

In the cauldron boil and bake;

Eye of newt and toe of frog,

Wool of bat and tongue of dog,

Adder's fork and blind-worm's sting,

Lizard's leg and owlet's wing,

For a charm of powerful trouble,

Like a hell-broth boil and bubble.

### All:

Double, double toil and trouble;

Fire burn; and cauldron bubble.

### Third Witch:

Scale of dragon, tooth of wolf,

Witches' mummy\*, maw and gulf

Of the ravined salt-sea shark.     *ravenous*

Root of hemlock digged in the dark,

*\*Dried human flesh used as the basis for a medicinal liquid!*

Liver of blaspheming Jew,

Gall of goat, and slips of yew

Silvered in the moon's eclipse,

Nose of Turk and Tartar's lips.

Finger of birth-strangled babe

Ditch-delivered by a drab,

Make the gruel thick and slab:

Add thereto a tiger's chaudron,         *entrails*

For the ingredients of our cauldron.

**All:**

Double, double toil and trouble;

Fire burn and cauldron bubble.

**Second Witch:**

Cool it with a baboon's blood,

Then the charm is firm and good.

*Enter HECATE, and another three witches*

**Hecate:**

O well done! I commend your pains,

And every one shall share in the gains;

And now about the cauldron sing,

Live elves and fairies in a ring,

Enchanting all that you put in.

*Music and a song, 'Black spirits', etc.*

*Exeunt HECATE and the three other witches.*

**Second Witch:**

By the pricking of my thumbs,

Something wicked this way comes.

*Knocking*

Open, locks,

Whoever knocks!

From *Macbeth*, Act 4, Scene 1

---

## Fast Facts

### Macbeth – 'the Scottish play'

*Macbeth* is a very dark play full of dark minds and extreme violence, including the murder of children. The spells incanted by the witches are based on actual witches' spells. And, because much of the play is in darkness, accidents backstage are common – it is alleged that on the first night of the first production of the play, the boy playing Lady Macbeth, Hal Berridge, died backstage. With all this in the background, it is hardly surprising actors are very superstitious about 'the Scottish play'!

Shakespeare used the image of a dagger in many of his plays as a symbol of treachery. In the second extract from *Macbeth* that follows below, from Act 2, Scene 1, Macbeth has a vision of a dagger which seems like a sign to him that he should use a dagger to murder King Duncan.

**Macbeth:**

Go bid thy mistress, when my drink is ready,
She strike upon the bell. Get thee to bed.

   *Exit servant*

Is this a dagger, which I see before me,
The handle toward my hand?
Come, let me clutch thee.
I have thee not, and yet I see thee still.
Art thou not, fatal vision, sensible
To feeling as to sight? or art thou but
A dagger of the mind, a false creation,
Proceeding from the heat-oppressed brain?
I see thee yet, in form as palpable    *able to be touched*
As this which now I draw.
Thou marshall'st me the way that I was going;    *guided*
And such an instrument I was to use.
Mine eyes are made the fools of the other senses,
Or else worth all the rest: I see thee still;
*handle* And on thy blade and dudgeon, gouts of blood,    *drops*

Which was not so before. There's no such thing.
It is the bloody business which informs
Thus to mine eyes. Now o'er the one half-world
Nature seems dead, and wicked dreams abuse
The curtained sleep: Witchcraft celebrates
Pale Hecate's* offerings, and withered Murther,     *murder*
Alarumed by his sentinel, the wolf,
Whose howl's his watch, thus with his stealthy
pace,
With Tarquin's** ravishing strides, towards his
design                                              *enterprise*
Moves like a ghost. Thou sure and firm-set earth,
Hear not my steps, which way they walk, for
fear
Thy very stones prate of my where-about,            *speak*
And take the present horror from the time,
Which now suits with it. Whiles I threat, he
lives:
Words to the heat of deeds too cold breath
gives.

   *A bell rings*

I go, and it is done: the bell invites me.
Hear it not, Duncan; for it is a knell      *the sound of a bell*
                                             *rung to announce*
That summons thee to Heaven or to Hell.          *a death*

*The goddess of the Moon **A Roman king

93

## King Richard III

*King Richard III* is set during the Wars of the Roses – a war between the houses of Lancaster and York. Richard, Duke of Gloucester and of the house of York, is determined to become king after the death of his brother Edward IV presently at death's door. First he murders his other brother, George, then he has Edward's two young sons locked in the tower. He says it is for their own safety but he then has them murdered before he is finally crowned King Richard III. Henry, Earl of Richmond and of the house of Lancaster, brings an army from France and defeats Richard at the Battle of Bosworth Field. As the battle draws to a climax Richard is unhorsed and utters the often-quoted line 'A horse! A horse! My kingdom for a horse!'

The Earl of Richmond slays Richard and is crowned King Henry VII, the first of the Tudor monarchs of the house of Lancaster.

Richard is an ugly hunchback, describing himself as 'rudely stamp'd' and 'deformed, unfinish'd', who cannot 'strut before a wanton ambling nymph' and in the speech below he reveals how jealous he is of his brother and how he plots to 'set my brother Clarence and the King in deadly hate, the one against the other.'

**Richard, Duke of Gloucester:**
Now is the winter of our discontent
Made glorious summer by this son of York;
And all the clouds that loured upon our House    *hung menacingly*
In the deep bosom of the ocean buried.
Now are our brows bound with victorious wreaths,
Our bruised arms hung up for monuments,
Our stern alarums changed to merry meetings,
Our dreadful marches to delightful measures.
*grim faced* Grim-visag'd War hath smoothed his wrinkled front:
And now, instead of mounting barbed steeds
To fright the souls of fearful adversaries,

He capers nimbly in a lady's chamber

*lustful*   To the lascivious pleasing of a lute.

But I, that am not shaped for sportive tricks,

Nor made to court an amorous looking-glass;

I, that am rudely stamped, and want love's majesty

To strut before a wanton ambling nymph:

I, that am curtailed of this fair proportion,

Cheated of feature by dissembling nature,

Deformed, unfinished, sent before my time

Into this breathing world, scarce half made up –

And that so lamely and unfashionable

That dogs bark at me, as I halt by them –

Why, I, in this weak piping time of peace,

Have no delight to pass away the time,

Unless to spy my shadow in the sun,

And descant on mine own deformity.

And therefore, since I cannot prove a lover

To entertain these fair well-spoken days,

I am determined to prove a villain,

And hate the idle pleasures of these days.

Plots have I laid, inductions dangerous,

By drunken prophecies, libels and dreams,

To set my brother Clarence and the King

In deadly hate, the one against the other:

And if King Edward be as true and just

As I am subtle, false, and treacherous,
This day should Clarence closely be mewed up *confined*
About a prophecy, which says that 'G'
Of Edward's heirs the murderer shall be –
Dive, thoughts, down to my soul: here
Clarence comes.

From *Richard III*, Act 1, Scene 1

## oɔ Fast Facts

### Richard **III** and physical deformity

In Elizabethan times, physical deformity was seen as punishment by God and the mark of a sinner. Richard's hunchback would therefore have marked him as evil. However, Shakespeare takes a more rational view and shows through Richard's own words that his evil comes about not through infirmity but by choice: *I am determined to prove a villain.*

The most likely reason that Shakespeare chose Richard as the subject for a play was because he was from the Plantagenet family and he had been defeated at the Battle of Bosworth by Henry Tudor, who then became King Henry VII, Queen Elizabeth's grandfather. The play would certainly have pleased her!

## The Merchant of Venice

Bassanio needs 3,000 ducats to court Portia and goes to his friend Antonio, the merchant in the play's title. Antonio does not have the money but as his ships are due back any day from a trading trip he soon will. He approaches the Jewish moneylender, Shylock, and asks for a short term loan to help his friend. Shylock, who has been badly insulted by Antonio before, agrees but only on condition that should things go wrong Antonio will have to pay him a pound of his flesh.

In the way of all good drama, the deal goes wrong when Antonio's ships are lost at sea and Shylock now wants his pound of flesh.

The day is saved by Portia who, dressed as a lawyer, says that Shylock can only have his pound of flesh provided no blood is drawn as this was not in the agreement. All ends well for everyone except Shylock.

While the play has an anti-Semitic (anti-Jewish) content it is hard to know what Shakespeare really thought as he does give Shylock some splendidly defensive lines, even if he does do him down in the end; however, the audiences of the day would not have accepted anything less since most believed in the religious teachings of the early church which encouraged the belief that the Jews had murdered Christ and were actively working to subvert the spread of Christianity. There is some evidence to suggest that Shakespeare was friendly with a woman of Jewish birth (the Dark Lady mentioned in some twenty-four of his sonnets) and this might explain his sympathy.

**Antonio:**

    Well, Shylock, shall we be beholding to you?

**Shylock:**

    Signior Antonio, many a time and oft
    In the Rialto you have rated me      *interest on*
    About my moneys and my usances:      *a loan*
    Still have I borne it with a patient shrug,

(For sufferance is the badge of all our tribe).
You call me misbeliever, cut-throat dog,
And spit upon my Jewish gaberdine,     *cloak*
And all for use of that which is mine own.
Well then, it now appears you need my help:
Go to, then; you come to me, and you say
'Shylock, we would have moneys,' you say so:
You, that did void your rheum upon my beard     *spit*
And foot me as you spurn a stranger cur     *dog*
Over your threshold: moneys is your suit.
What should I say to you? Should I not say
'Hath a dog money? is it possible
A cur can lend three thousand ducats?' Or
Shall I bend low and in a bondman's key
With bated breath, and whispering humbleness,
Say this:
'Fair sir, you spit on me on Wednesday last;
You spurn'd me such a day; another time
You called me dog: and for these courtesies
I'll lend you thus much moneys?'

**Antonio:**

I am as like to call thee so again,
To spit on thee again, to spurn thee too.
If thou wilt lend this money, lend it not

As to thy friends, for when did friendship take
A breed for barren metal of his friend?
But lend it rather to thine enemy,
Who, if he break, thou mayst with better face
Exact the penalty.

From *The Merchant of Venice*, Act 1, Scene 3

 **Fast Facts**

## Shakespeare and the Jews

Hundreds of years before the Nazi holocaust, Jews were being sidelined, abused and murdered, but it was for religious reasons and not because of race. Anti-Semitism was rife in England and across the whole of Christian Europe in the time of Shakespeare, because Jews were regarded as being responsible for the death of Christ. Although they were banned from living in England, there were people of the Jewish race in the country who were Christianised. But even they were often persecuted because they were thought to practice the Jewish faith in secret.

So was Shakespeare anti-Semitic? There is no easy answer. Sometimes the characters in *The Merchant of Venice* certainly reflect the prejudices of the time but Shakespeare does give Shylock some truly great speeches to defend his faith, so it is possible he was sympathetic or at least neutral to the plight of the Jews.

## Romeo and Juliet

The love story to end all love stories, *Romeo and Juliet* is about the children of two warring families, Romeo Montague and Juliet Capulet, who meet, fall in love and are secretly married. A plan is hatched to allow the young lovers to be together but it goes horribly wrong when Romeo finds out that Juliet is apparently dead and in grief kills himself with poison. Juliet, however, is only drugged to make her appear dead and wakes to find her lifeless husband beside her. In despair, she then kills herself with a dagger. The war between the Montagues and Capulets ends.

Baz Luhrmann's film of *Romeo and Juliet*, starring Leonardo DiCaprio and Claire Danes, is set in modern-day California but with Shakespeare's original dialogue. This movie is really worth watching as is the musical, *West Side Story*, also based on Shakespeare's *Romeo and Juliet*.

**Romeo:**

He jests at scars that never felt a wound.

*Juliet appears above (at a window)*

But soft, what light through yonder window breaks?

It is the east, and Juliet is the sun!

Arise, fair sun, and kill the envious moon

Who is already sick and pale with grief

That thou her maid art far more fair than she.

Be not her maid, since she is envious,

Her vestal livery is but sick and green     *virgin's clothes*

And none but fools do wear it. Cast it off.

It is my lady, O it is my love!

O that she knew she were!

She speaks, yet she says nothing. What of that?

Her eye discourses, I will answer it.     *speaks*

I am too bold. 'Tis not to me she speaks.

Two of the fairest stars in all the heaven,
Having some business, do entreat her eyes
To twinkle in their spheres till they return.
What if her eyes were there, they in her
head?
The brightness of her cheek would shame
those stars,
As daylight doth a lamp; her eyes in heaven
Would through the airy region stream so
bright
That birds would sing and think it were not
night.
See how she leans her cheek upon her hand.
O that I were a glove upon that hand,
That I might touch that cheek!

**Juliet:**

Ay me.

**Romeo:**

She speaks.
O speak again bright angel, for thou art
As glorious to this night, being o'er my head,
As is a winged messenger of heaven
Unto the white-upturned wondering eyes
Of mortals that fall back to gaze on him

When he bestrides the lazy-puffing clouds
And sails upon the bosom of the air.

**Juliet:**

O Romeo, Romeo, wherefore art thou Romeo?
Deny thy father and refuse thy name,
Or if thou wilt not, be but sworn my love
And I'll no longer be a Capulet.

From *Romeo and Juliet*, Act 2, Scene 2

## King Henry V

King Henry is about to tax the church to pay for wars and the poor. To head him off, the church gives him money to go and fight for the crown of France. In France, he battles and finally succeeds in taking the French town of Halfleurs. Later he takes on the might of the French, five to one against, and soundly defeats them at the Battle of Agincourt.

Two of Shakespeare's truly great heroic speeches are in this play: 'Once more unto the breach . . .' and what is usually called the 'St Crispin's Day speech'. Both are included below.

If you listen to the pre-battle speeches of Aragorn and Theoden King in *Lord of the Rings*, you will hear how Shakespeare's words have influenced them. The first speech is from Act 3, Scene 1.

**King Henry V:**

Once more unto the breach, dear friends, once more,

Or close the wall up with our English dead.

In peace there's nothing so becomes a man

As modest stillness and humility;
But when the blast of war blows in our ears,
Then imitate the action of the tiger:
Stiffen the sinews, conjure up the blood,
Disguise fair nature with hard-favoured rage.
Then lend the eye a terrible aspect;
Let it pry through the portage of the head
Like the brass cannon; let the brow o'erwhelm
it
As fearfully as doth a galled rock            *worn*
O'erhang and jutty his confounded base,
Swilled with the wild and wasteful ocean.
Now set the teeth and stretch the nostril
wide,
Hold hard the breath and bend up every spirit
To his full height. On, on, you noble English,
Whose blood is fet from fathers of war-proof,
Fathers that like so many Alexanders
Have in these parts from morn till even
fought,
And sheathed their swords for lack of
argument.
Dishonour not your mothers; now attest
That those whom you called fathers did beget
you.
Be copy now to men of grosser blood

And teach them how to war. And you, good
yeomen,
Whose limbs were made in England, show us
here
The mettle of your pasture; let us swear
That you are worth your breeding – which I
doubt not,
For there is none of you so mean and base,
That hath not noble lustre in your eyes.
I see you stand like greyhounds in the slips,
Straining upon the start. The game's afoot.
Follow your spirit, and upon this charge
Cry 'God for Harry! England and Saint George!'

The second speech is from Act 4, Scene 3.

**King Henry V:**

. . . he which hath no stomach to this fight,
Let him depart; his passport shall be made
And crowns for convoy put into his purse.
We would not die in that man's company
That fears his fellowship to die with us.
This day is called the feast of Crispian.
He that outlives this day and comes safe home
Will stand a-tiptoe when the day is named
And rouse him at the name of Crispian.
He that shall live this day, and see old age,

Will yearly on the vigil feast his neighbours,
And say 'Tomorrow is Saint Crispian.'
Then will he strip his sleeve and show his scars,
And say 'These wounds I had on Crispin's day.'
Old men forget; yet all shall be forgot,
But he'll remember, with advantages,
What feats he did that day: then shall our names,
Familiar in his mouth as household words,
Harry the King, Bedford and Exeter,
Warwick and Talbot, Salisbury and Gloucester,
Be in their flowing cups freshly remembered.
This story shall the good man teach his son;
And Crispin Crispian shall ne'er go by,
From this day to the ending of the world,
But we in it shall be remembered,
We few, we happy few, we band of brothers.
For he today that sheds his blood with me
Shall be my brother; be he ne'er so vile,
This day shall gentle his condition.
And gentlemen in England now abed
Shall think themselves accursed they were not here,
And hold their manhoods cheap whiles any speaks
That fought with us upon Saint Crispin's day.

## *Twelfth Night*

Another woman-dressed-as-a-man caper from Mr S! This time a ship is wrecked on the coast of Illyria (see the end of the movie, *Shakespeare in Love*) and Viola is washed ashore assuming her twin brother Sebastian has been lost. Disguising herself as a boy called Cesario she gets a job as a page (servant) to Duke Orsino. Though apparently a boy, Viola/Cesario falls in love with Orsino, but Orsino wishes to marry Olivia and so sends Viola/Cesario to woo her on his behalf. Olivia falls for Cesario, who, of course, is Viola (are you still with me?).

In the end Viola gets Orsino and Olivia gets Sebastian, Viola's twin and lookalike (as Cesario). There's more to it, of course, but I've probably confused you enough! It makes sense when you see the play!

**Duke Orsino:**

If music be the food of love, play on,
Give me excess of it, that, surfeiting,          *taking too much*
The appetite may sicken, and so die.
That strain again, it had a dying fall:
O, it came o'er my ear like the sweet sound,
That breathes upon a bank of violets,
Stealing and giving odour. Enough, no more;
'Tis not so sweet now as it was before.
O spirit of love, how quick and fresh art thou,
That notwithstanding thy capacity
Receiveth as the sea, nought enters there,
Of what validity and pitch soe'er,
But falls into abatement and low price,          *a diminished amount*
Even in a minute! So full of shapes is fancy,
That it alone is high fantastical.

From *Twelfth Night*, Act 1 , Scene 1

## The Tempest

Prospero was once the Duke of Milan but he was usurped by his brother Antonio. Prospero now lives on an island where he has studied magic. With him are his daughter Miranda and his two slaves, the savage creature, Caliban, and the spirit, Ariel.

When King Alonso and his sons, Ferdinand and Antonio, are shipwrecked on the island the fun and fireworks begin as people fall in love, plot to kill and have a fantastical time.

In the end boy gets girl, that is Ferdinand gets Miranda, and everyone else makes up.

Lovely stuff!

**Prospero:**

You do look, my son, in a moved sort,
As if you were dismay'd. Be cheerful, sir.
Our revels now are ended. These our actors, *merry-making*
As I foretold you, were all spirits and
Are melted into air, into thin air;
And – like the baseless fabric of this vision –
The cloud-capp'd towers, the gorgeous palaces,
The solemn temples, the great globe itself,
Yea, all which it inherit, shall dissolve,
And, like this insubstantial pageant faded,
Leave not a rack behind. We are such stuff
As dreams are made on, and our little life
Is rounded with a sleep.

From *The Tempest*, Act 4, Scene 1

## King John

More wars and religious intrigue end in the murder of King John by a monk. The play is noteworthy for the following piece which is all the more powerful when you realise that Shakespeare's own son Hamnet died of the plague in 1596 at the age of eleven. You can feel the heartbreak in every word in this extract from Act 3, Scene 3.

**Constance:**

Grief fills the room up of my absent child,
Lies in his bed, walks up and down with me,
Puts on his pretty looks, repeats his words,
Remembers me of all his gracious parts,
Stuffs out his vacant garments with his form;
Then, have I reason to be fond of grief?
Fare you well: had you such a loss as I,
I could give better comfort than you do.
I will not keep this form upon my head,
When there is such disorder in my wit.
O Lord! my boy, my Arthur, my fair son!
My life, my joy, my food, my all the world!
My widow-comfort, and my sorrows' cure!

## *King Lear*

King Lear is getting old and wants to divide his kingdom between his three daughters, Goneril, Regan and Cordelia. In a fit of vanity, he decides that his kingdom will be divided according to how much they love him.

Goneril and Regan go over the top in expressing their love while Cordelia will not pander to his vanity and says she loves him as a daughter should. For this she is disinherited.

So begins a series of tragic and bloody events involving sister killing sister and madness that lead to the death of Lear and his daughters.

This tragedy is thought by some to be Shakespeare's greatest play.

**King Lear:**

Blow winds and crack your cheeks! Rage, blow!
You cataracts and hurricanoes, spout          *waterfalls*
Till you have drench'd our steeples, drowned
the cocks!
You sulphurous and thought-executing fires,
Vaunt-couriers of oak-cleaving thunderbolts,*forerunners*

Singe my white head! And thou, all-shaking thunder,
Smite flat the thick rotundity of the world,
Crack nature's moulds, all germens spill at once
That make ingrateful man!

From *King Lear*, Act 3, Scene 2

## ⊙⊙ Fast Facts

### Too much violence?

Shakespeare's plays are full of violence and for good reason: it was very much part of the times and his audiences would have expected no less. Hangings and beheadings were carried out in public and attracted large audiences. Those who lost their heads had them stuck on top of a pole and placed on London Bridge for all to see; the hanged were left to rot on the gallows.

It is worth noting that *Titus Andronicus*, probably Shakespeare's most brutal play, was put on in Poland – a country savaged by the Nazis – at the end of World War II to great acclaim. We live in thankfully gentler times and therefore tend to find the brutality of Shakespeare's times distasteful.

## Othello

Othello the Moor has gone to fight the Turks in Cyprus and takes his wife Desdemona with him. Iago, a standard bearer, sets about scheming the downfall of the Moor by planting Desdemona's handkerchief on Cassio, Othello's best friend.

Othello immediately suspects that Cassio and Desdemona are having an affair and overcome with jealousy he smothers Desdemona.

In the end Iago's wife, Emilia, exposes the plot and is murdered by Iago. Distraught with grief, Othello commits suicide and Iago, we assume, is taken away, tortured and executed.

If much of Shakespeare's tragedies seems 'over the top', just study the history of the time and you will see that such things were not uncommon.

What Iago says below is quite true – your good name is more important than riches – but as one of the most diabolical villains in Shakespeare's plays, he is full of hypocrisy when he says it.

**Iago:**

Good name in man and woman, dear my lord,
Is the immediate jewel of their souls:
Who steals my purse steals trash – 'tis something – nothing;
'Twas mine, 'tis his, and has been slave to thousands –
But he that filches from me my good name    *steals*
Robs me of that which not enriches him
And makes me poor indeed.

From *Othello*, Act 3, Scene 3

## King Richard II

Henry Bolingbroke has accused Thomas Mowbray of squandering money given to him for the king's soldiers and there is also concern over the recent, mysterious death of the Duke of Gloucester. Both men want King Richard to act as judge in the matter. Richard is unable to do so and instead he banishes both men from England.

When Bolingbroke's father, John of Gaunt, dies, Richard seizes his land and money to fund a war in Ireland which angers the nobility. With their assistance, Bolingbroke returns and is crowned Henry IV. When Richard returns from administering the war in Ireland, he is imprisoned and murdered.

The speech below from Act 2, Scene 1 delivers one of the great songs of praise to England which is often quoted to this day.

**John of Gaunt:**

> Methinks I am a prophet new inspired,
> And thus expiring do foretell of him:
> His rash fierce blaze of riot cannot last,
> For violent fires soon burn out themselves;

Small showers last long, but sudden storms
are short;
He tires betimes that spurs too fast betimes;
With eager feeding food doth choke the
feeder;
Light vanity, insatiate cormorant,          *greedy*
Consuming means, soon preys upon itself.
This royal throne of kings, this sceptered isle,
This earth of majesty, this seat of Mars,
This other Eden, demi-paradise,
This fortress built by Nature for herself
Against infection and the hand of war,
This happy breed of men, this little world,
This precious stone set in the silver sea,
Which serves it in the office of a wall,
Or as a moat defensive to a house,
Against the envy of less happier lands.

This blessed plot, this earth, this realm, this England,
This nurse, this teeming womb of royal kings,
Feared by their breed and famous by their birth,
Renowned for their deeds as far from home,
For Christian service and true chivalry,
As is the sepulchre in stubborn Jewry,
Of the world's ransom, blessed Mary's Son;
This land of such dear souls, this dear dear land,
Dear for her reputation through the world,
Is now leased out – I die pronouncing it –
Like to a tenement or pelting farm.    *worthless/small*
England, bound in with the triumphant sea,
Whose rocky shore beats back the envious siege
Of watery Neptune, is now bound in with shame,
With inky blots and rotten parchment bonds;
That England, that was wont to conquer others,
Hath made a shameful conquest of itself.
Ah, would the scandal vanish with my life,
How happy then were my ensuing death!

# SHAKESPEARE COUNTRY

## The Birthplace, Henley Street, Stratford-upon-Avon, Warwickshire

This is the house that John Shakespeare purchased, probably in two stages in 1556 and 1575. It is generally accepted as being the place where Young William and his brothers and sisters were born and grew up. It includes the birth room where it is suggested he was actually born.

The house has gone through many uses since Shakespeare's time including a tavern. It has now been restored. Beside it is the premises of the Birthplace Trust which contains many records and artefacts from the time of Shakespeare.

## Anne Hathaway's Cottage, Shottery, Stratford-upon-Avon

This was the childhood home and probable birthplace of Anne Hathaway, wife of William Shakespeare. Anne's father was a yeoman farmer and the 'cottage' was quite a large residence. It is situated in the village of Shottery about a mile from the Stratford town centre.

Today most of the land between the cottage and the town centre has been built over but in Shakespeare's day there would have been open fields between the two. It is now owned by the Shakespeare Birthplace Trust.

## Mary Arden's House and Shakespeare Country Museum

Mary Arden was the wife of John Shakespeare and the mother of William Shakespeare. She was the daughter of Robert Arden, a successful husbandman (farmer) with eight daughters from his first marriage. Mary would have grown up in the Arden's family home, later known as Glebe Farm, in the small village of Wilmcote near Stratford.

The name Mary Arden's House was first given to a timber-framed farmhouse in Wilmcote, which now houses part of the Shakespeare Countryside Museum and is called Palmer's Farm. However, quite recently the true location of the Arden homestead was found to be the neighbouring Glebe Farm which is now owned by the Shakespeare Birthplace Trust and is correctly known as Mary Arden's House.

## Hall's Croft, Old Town, Stratford-upon-Avon

Hall's Croft was the home of Dr John Hall, Shakespeare's physician and the husband of Shakespeare's daughter Susanna. A Tudor building, it contains Tudor and Jacobean furniture as well as an exhibition on Tudor medicine.

## New Place and Nash's House, Stratford-upon-Avon

New Place was Shakespeare's family home in Stratford-upon-Avon from 1597. He lived there when not in London and it is where he died in 1616. Although it has been levelled, the foundations still remain, as does his garden containing plants of the time and a geometric Knott Garden. A well has also survived which originally lay in a courtyard surrounded by buildings at the back of the Shakespeare's five-bay timbered house.

Adjacent to New Place is Nash's House, named after Thomas Nash who owned it. Nash was the first husband of Shakespeare's granddaughter Elizabeth. Nash's House now contains a display illustrating Stratford's local history and is furnished as it would have been in Nash's day.

## King Edward VI Grammar School, Stratford-upon-Avon

King Edward VI Grammar School is still a working school to this day. Established by the Guild of the Holy Cross, the school can trace its origins to 1295. Edward VI assured the future of the school when he placed the old Guild properties into the care of the townspeople in 1553.

The Protestant King Edward VI would have wished the school to create educated young men who could translate the Bible and achieve the high ideals of Christian living.

Although there is no actual proof that Shakespeare attended this school it would probably be absurd to think otherwise. It was his local school and his ability as a writer was almost certainly polished and perfected here.

## Globe Theatre, London

The Globe Theatre was first built in 1599 by the company of players to which William Shakespeare belonged. It was destroyed by fire in 1613 and rebuilt in 1614. Due to the growth of Puritanism it was closed in 1642 and demolished in 1644.

Through the dedication of American playwright Sam Wanamaker, a modern reconstruction opened in London in 1997, two hundred yards away from the original site.

## Holy Trinity Church

This is the church in Stratford-upon-Avon where Shakespeare was baptised on 23 April 1564, and the one he would have attended as a child. He was buried here on 23 April 1616.

His self-penned epitaph reads:

Good friend for Jesus sake forbeare,
To dig the dust enclosed here.
Blessed be the man that spares these stones,
And cursed be he that moves my bones.

# THE WORKS OF
# SHAKESPEARE

## Tragedies

*Antony and Cleopatra*
*Coriolanus*
*Hamlet*
*Julius Caesar*
*King Lear*
*Macbeth*
*Othello*
*Romeo and Juliet*
*Timon of Athens*
*Titus Andronicus*

## Histories

*King Henry IV, Part I*
*King Henry IV, Part II*
*King Henry V*
*King Henry VI, Part I*
*King Henry VI, Part II*
*King Henry VI, Part III*
*King Henry VIII*
*King John*
*King Richard II*
*King Richard III*

## Comedies

*All's Well That Ends Well*
*As you Like It*
*The Comedy of Errors*
*Cymbeline*
*Love's Labour's Lost*
*Measure for Measure*
*The Merry Wives of Windsor*
*The Merchant of Venice*
*A Midsummer Night's Dream*
*Much Ado About Nothing*
*Pericles, Prince of Tyre*
*The Taming of the Shrew*
*The Tempest*
*Troilius and Cressida*
*Twelfth Night*
*Two Gentlemen of Verona*
*A Winter's Tale*

## Poetry

*The Sonnets*
*A Lover's Complaint*
*The Rape of Lucrece*
*Venus and Adonis*